P**I**NK BAT

Turning Problems Into Solutions

Michael McMillan

This book is dedicated to all the unique characters

I grew up with and to all those I've met along the way...

and plan to meet in the future. Thank you.

People asking questions... lost in confusion,

Well, I tell them there's no problem... only solutions.

—John Lennon

Table of Contents

Everywhere you look today there are problems.

Turn on your TV or computer—pick up a magazine

or paper—and what do you see? Problems!

Talk to your spouse, co-workers, family members or

friends, and within minutes someone will bring up a

problem... or two or three.

Problems permeate the workplace, too—new products,

old products, customer service, health care, retirement

plans, sales, marketing, budgets, IT, personnel—

the list of problems we confront each day is vast.

If that's not enough, consider the global problems we are facing—hunger, war, terrorism, economy, jobs, pollution, global climate change, disease, energy, health care, education, government corruption, trade barriers, overpopulation, sanitation, water—the world's problems seem endless.

In short, we are experiencing a "problem pandemic" like never before. What's scarier yet, is many experts predict there is no end in sight. So what can YOU do about this threatening pandemic?

Embrace it! This may seem strange at first, but by
the time you finish reading this book, you will realize
many "problems" aren't problems at all. In fact, most
problems are opportunities and many are actually
Pink Bats—unseen solutions just waiting to be found.

Can you imagine waking up each morning faced
with a "solution pandemic"?

Start imagining. Maybe you think this idea seems
impossible, but you're about to discover:

"Pink Bat Thinking" makes the impossible possible.

The **PINK BAT** Story

Growing up, the kids in my neighborhood loved

playing baseball. During summer vacations, whenever

possible, we would form a game in someone's back

yard—often playing until dark.

As we grew, so did the number

of broken windows and screens. Eventually our

parents got together and banned backyard baseball!

For a group of baseball loving kids, their solution

became our problem.

One day, my neighbor Gary and I were sitting at my picnic table trading baseball cards and lamenting. We couldn't really blame our parents for banning backyard baseball, especially in front of Gary—it was his dad that organized the ban. Truth be told, I didn't blame him either.

If a foul ball had crashed through our window and landed on the kitchen table during dinner, my dad probably would have done the same. While the problem seemed obvious, the solution didn't.

"I know… we could play at the park," I suggested.

"No… it's too far. Besides, the high school team practices there,"

Gary responded.

"What about wiffle ball?"

"No way… wiffle ball is stupid!"

Before I could make another suggestion for Gary to shut

down, our friend Doug pulled up on his bike, looking like

the cat that had swallowed the canary. *"Hey guys, check it out!"*

Doug said, holding a softball-sized rubber ball over his head.

"They banned hardball, but nobody said a word about this,"

he continued, tossing the ball to Gary.

Doug had a point. None of us could remember any rubber

ball discussions, warnings or bans mentioned.

"Where'd you get this thing?" Gary asked.

"It's disgusting… it looks like it was a dog's ball," he continued.

Doug's smirk reappeared, *"It was my dog's ball."*

*"**You stole Lady's ball?**"* I said in disbelief. Doug's dog was fourteen years old, blind, and could barely walk. Stealing her ball didn't seem right on any level.

*"**No, I borrowed it,**"* Doug responded. *"**Besides she stopped playing with it months ago.**"*

*"**I can see why,**"* Gary said, holding it between his thumb and finger like a big rotten tomato.

Regardless of where the ball came from or why, if there was a chance of playing backyard baseball again, we were willing to give it a try.

Since it was just the three of us, we agreed to take turns batting, pitching and fielding. Doug took the mound and Gary stepped up to the garbage-can-lid home plate. Being the youngest, I took my position out deep in center field, where Mom's garden bordered the neighbor's fence.

Doug went into his windup and delivered an irresistible pitch that Gary jacked over my head, Mom's garden, and the fence. Then it deflected off Rat Newman's window and landed in his back yard!

Gary strutted to first base with his arms victoriously

raised, then jogged around the infield before crossing

home. *"Hey, hey... it works! I love this ball, Doug...*

what a great idea!"

"Since you love it so much, why don't you climb Rat's fence and

get it?" I yelled from deep center field.

"Because I'm not playing outfield… you are!"

"Those are the rules," Doug added. *"Just go get the ball, Mikey."*

Doug made up all the rules. He changed them, too.

I remember my first home run. As the ball flew over the

fence, Doug suddenly recalled a rule he had somehow

forgotten. ***"Home run balls must be retrieved by the player***

responsible for hitting them!" he stated authoritatively.

Interestingly, this rule only applied to me. Why?

Because, according to Doug, ***"the youngest player must***

fetch the ball" rule, trumps it. He said it was a technicality

but that someday, when a younger kid took my spot, I

would appreciate it.

I climbed the Newmans' fence and landed in their back
yard only to find Rat dressed in a shiny homemade space
suit, running with his arms stretched out like an airplane.
Rat was a year older than me—a skinny kid with a pointed
nose who didn't care much for playing baseball.

"Hi Rat," I said as I searched for the ball. *"Did you happen to see
a ball land in your yard?"*

Rat nodded and continued 'flying' in circles. *"Are you referring
to the projectile that entered my orbital pattern?"*

"Yeah, I guess."

With that, Rat broke from his orbit and flew over

toward the bushes, circled the ball three times, then

returned to his original pattern.

I thanked him, walked over, and picked up the ball.

"Hey Rat, we could use another player... do you wanna play?"

Rat stopped and hovered for a moment. *"Thanks, Michael,*

but no thanks. My mission must be completed by sunset."

As I climbed back over the fence, Rat climbed into

his homemade spacecraft, a modified garbage can, and

started speaking into a tinfoil microphone.

After several pitches, we concluded that Doug's "great"

solution wasn't so great after all... at least I reached

this conclusion. Every other pitch ended up in the

Newmans' back yard. As the designated fence climber,

I considered this to be a definite problem.

I'm still not certain what was worse... listening to

Gary yell "Hey, hey," climbing the Newmans' fence

for the umpteenth time, or interrupting Rat's mission

so he could help me find the projectile that kept

violating his airspace.

To add insult to injury, after returning from my fifth trip,

Gary yelled, *"Hey, Mikey, what's taking you so long?*

Are you and your buddy playing spaceships? We were

beginning to think a UFO abducted you!"

"Real funny. This ball isn't working, you guys…

it's a problem," I said.

"A problem? This ball is great!" Gary responded, *"and it doesn't*

break stuff," he added to support his claim.

Then I had an idea…

Maybe the problem

vasn't the ball at all!

"I'll be right back," I said as I ran to the back steps, flung

open the door, and dashed down the basement stairs.

Then I began rummaging through a large cabinet filled

with old baby clothes, decorations and toys—junk—

until I found it! It looked even more childish than I

had remembered. The package had a picture of a bright

red plastic bat and read, "My First Swing—For ages 3

and up." Then I noticed the tag hanging from the bow:

"To Michael: Happy #9.

I hope you have a special day and enjoy your gift!

Love, Grandma."

I didn't have the heart to tell her it was a toy for toddlers.

I just hugged her and thanked her for the gift.

After she left, I put it in the basement along with the

other stuff my family somehow couldn't give away—

or throw away.

When I re-emerged, Doug and Gary were playing catch.

"Hey guys, maybe this will work," I said, holding the box

above my head.

"What is it?" Gary asked with a peculiar look on his face.

"A bat," I said. *"Let's try it out!"*

To say Doug and Gary were entertained by watching me

rip open the box and pull out the fat, shiny, red plastic

bat would be an understatement.

They were laughing hysterically.

"That's a bat for babies!" Doug said, holding his stomach.

"Mikey still is a baby," Gary added, *"and I'm not playing with his baby bat!"*

I walked toward the plate. *"Come on… just pitch it to me."*

"Fine," Doug said, *"But you look like an idiot."*

"He is an idiot," Gary added, still unable to stop himself from laughing.

Doug took the mound and I stepped into the pretend

batter's box, firmly gripping the red bat and cocking

my elbow in anticipation.

"All right, Mikey, pull up your diaper and be ready. I'll tell you

when to swing," Doug said in a mocking voice.

Then he tossed a pitch right down the center of the

plate and I blasted a solid shot over his head and into

shallow center.

Gary and Doug stopped laughing as I ran to first base.

"See, it works! A perfect bat for backyard baseball!"

"Well, go get it, Gary!" Doug yelled.

"No way… it's still my turn to bat!" was Gary's reply.

It seemed we had

backyard bat and

Eventually, the backyard

and we wer

discovered the perfect

all combination.

aseball ban was lifted

ack in business...

After weeks of hard play, the sun and elements had gradually transformed my bat from bright red to a pale pink. We had been so busy playing, no one even noticed. In our minds, it was still the best red plastic bat in the world. Besides, whatever it may have lost in luster, it had gained in popularity. Like a magnet, the pink bat attracted kids from all around town. Eventually, so many kids showed up to play we needed more room. So we started playing at the schoolyard several blocks from our neighborhood.

One hot afternoon we had entered extra innings.

I was up to bat with a full count and two outs.

Doug was furiously chewing gum and concentrating

on delivering a pitch to end the inning.

"Drive me home, Mike!" the winning runner on

third yelled.

Doug rocked back and fired a fastball, waist high,

coming right down the middle. I swung with all

my power.

A loud crack echoed over the field and I took off running... but stopped halfway to first base. Blocking the sun with my hand, I watched as everyone stood staring up into the sky. Doug started kicking the grass and scanning the ground around his feet while others looked at one another in astonishment.

The ball had

vanished!!!!!!!!!!

"Where did it go?" I yelled out.

Gary shrugged as others continued glancing up and around the field for the answer. Aside from the birds, the schoolyard was silent.

Then a voice from the sky echoed out... *"THE BAT!!!"*

We all glanced up and around. Nobody said what everyone thought—was this the voice of God?

"What... who said that?" I asked, sounding about as confident as the Cowardly Lion did standing before the great and powerful Wizard of Oz.

"ME... up here!" the voice responded.

It wasn't the voice of God. It was Rat Newman who

had climbed up an old elm tree behind the backstop.

High above the crowd in his spacesuit, Rat clung to

a limb with one hand while holding a tinfoil ray gun

with the other.

"Rat... is that you?" I inquired.

"Yeah. Look inside... inside the pink bat," he said,

pointing toward home plate with his ray gun.

Until that moment, none of us had realized the bat

was no longer red... let alone pink!

Gary picked up the pink bat and rattled it.

Sure enough, the seam had split and the ball

was trapped inside it.

Doug and I jogged in to assess the situation.

As the others gathered around and looked over our

shoulders, we carefully spread the seam open like a

team of skilled surgeons and removed the ball.

The procedure was invasive, but we accomplished

the objective and our pink patient survived.

"Now what?" Gary said, running his finger along the split seam.

"We'll just have to be more careful and use the good side from now on," I replied.

Then I rotated the split seam to the back and returned to the plate. The other kids took their positions and the game continued.

We won the game, but the pink bat had been damaged in the process.

That night Doug stopped by and we tried everything

we could think of to fix it—scotch tape, duct tape,

glue and string—but nothing worked. After Doug

went home, I even tried band-aids… no luck.

We had a serious problem. Rotating the torn seam to the back was the only solution we found that worked. And it did work for a while. But all good things must come to an end, and the day we had all dreaded finally arrived. The second seam split and put an end to the pink bat—for good. Our golden goose was dead.

I can still picture the look on Gary's face as he stared mournfully, holding the pink bat in his hands.

"I think I killed it," he said, trying not to appear too upset.

"Well, it was bound to happen," I said. *"It was just a matter of time."*

"Maybe so, but what are we supposed to play with now?"

Doug asked.

"I don't know… but I'm sure we'll think of something."

In truth, I hadn't a clue of what that "something" might be.

I couldn't imagine anything replacing the pink bat…

I was still in denial.

After Gary dropped the pink bat, I picked it up,

hoping an idea would strike me as to how I might be

able to fix it. But that didn't happen. What did strike

me was anger, then sadness. I climbed on my bike

and headed for home. As I pedaled, I glanced down

at the weathered gift my grandma had given me

and reflected on all the good times it had provided.

To think I was once embarrassed by it and considered

it a problem. Doug, Gary and others had actually

laughed at it. Nobody was laughing now.

Mostly I thought about my grandma and how easy it is to take people and gifts for granted—until they're gone. Joni Mitchell is right, *"Don't it always seem to go that you don't know what you've got till it's gone."*

I arrived home to find the garbage can had

already been taken out to the curb. Having already

experienced the first four stages of grief—denial,

anger, bargaining and depression—I was ready to

accept the reality of the situation.

I took one long last look at the pink bat before

carefully placing it into the can.

That afternoon, we went in search of a replacement

bat with Doug's paper route money. We rode our

bikes to every store... no luck.

We still had a couple weeks before school started and

planned to spend each remaining day playing baseball.

We needed a new solution... and fast.

I searched the house and garage high and low for a

pink bat replacement. I grabbed an old wooden bat

and anything else I thought might work, including a

tennis racket, broom, and a large cardboard tube.

Armed with an arsenal of 'bats,' I rode my bike to the

schoolyard to try them out before anyone else arrived.

To my surprise, when I reached the schoolyard I

discovered a dozen or so kids were already on the field,

huddled around the pitcher's mound.

I parked my bike and went to see what was going

on. As I approached, the crowd slowly opened up to

reveal none other than... Rat Newman!

And of all things, he was holding the..

PINK BAT!

I couldn't believe my eyes. There he was... standing

in the center of the crowd, dressed in his spacesuit...

holding the pink bat above his head.

Rat looked like a wizard from another planet, casting

spells on his earthly followers with a big pink wand.

If that weren't enough, I couldn't believe my ears either.

"All right... listen up," Rat announced. *"I'm only repeating the rules once more! If the ball goes partway into the bat, that's a single. If it goes completely inside, you're out... period. If the ball enters one side and leaves through the other, it's a home run. Ok?"*

Just then, Rat looked up and noticed me standing there... with my jaw dropped and eyes wide open.

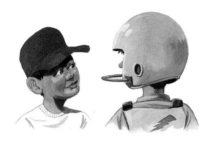

"Hey, Michael, want to play the new Pink Bat Game?"

Not knowing what to say or do, I smiled and said,

"Okay... sure, Rat!"

Then I walked over and joined the group of eager

kids and waited for my turn to play.

"Rat's Pink Bat Game" (as it came to be known) changed our reality. As a result, the pink bat remained popular for the rest of the summer. A few other things changed as well. I started playing infield and Doug lost his status as sole rule maker. While Rat was open to new ideas, no rules were modified without his consent... and even then... only if they improved the game. After all, he had created the game. Unless you have a better idea, it's hard to trump the creator.

What we learned that summer is that creativity is the most powerful force in the world. It can change reality.

Each day we played "Rat's Pink Bat Game," I wondered to myself, "Why didn't I think of that idea? Was I blind? Had my imagination stopped working?" In many ways, the answer to these questions is "Yes."

We've all heard the expression: "One man's junk is another man's treasure." Consider this: ***"One man's PROBLEM is another man's SOLUTION."*** If Rat could take a discarded bat (perceived problem) and turn it into an exciting new game (solution), then what's stopping YOU or me from doing the same?

Can you recall a specific time when a solution stared

you right in the face, yet somehow you missed it?

It always seems amazing after the fact, doesn't it?

We've all missed Pink Bat solutions before... it's more

common than not. So how do we start seeing the

endless solutions that surround us each and every day?

Before answering that question, let's understand how

we miss them in the first place. In part, it's due to a

phenomenon psychologists call "perceptual blindness"

or "inattentional blindness."

Consider the following example:

Professor Daniel Simons and his psychology students asked volunteers to watch a short video. In the video, team members (one team in black shirts, the other in white shirts) passed a basketball back and forth. Each volunteer was told to count the number of passes made by the team wearing white. At some point, a person in a gorilla suit appeared (for several seconds) during the video. When the video ended, the researchers asked if anybody had seen anything unusual. Only half of the volunteers reported seeing the gorilla; the others saw nothing unusual.

How could people not notice the gorilla in the room?

Mostly because they weren't looking for it. They were

focused on something else.

This explains how experts can be more susceptible

to perceptual blindness than beginners, and why

"outsiders" often find solutions that experienced

"insiders" miss. Beginners and outsiders are open to

possibilities and don't make assumptions. By extension,

they're often better at finding solutions the experts

have stopped seeing. Remember, Rat rarely played

baseball with us... he didn't share our bias.

Perceptual blindness sheds much light on why we miss obvious solutions. By focusing on one thing (a problem), we miss something else (a solution). Magicians and politicians have known about this phenomenon for years.

Labels reinforce this condition, too. When the pink bat split, we labeled it a problem... so it became one and we couldn't see it as anything else. Labels exist everywhere and often carry perceptions that are misleading.

Rat didn't label the pink bat as junk, broken, or useless. He saw it for what it was and focused on what it could be.

Our five senses collect far more input than we can ever process. To prevent sensory overload, our brain filters and edits the outside world. Through this selection process, our perception of reality is established and maintained. In other words, our reality is a filtered version of REALITY itself.

Subconsciously, our brain selects what we believe is possible, plausible and "real," while ignoring or blocking everything else. Have you ever been in a noisy room with many conversations going on at once when out of nowhere you hear your name mentioned?

That's your filter at work. Since you consider your name to be important, your brain filters out the less important information and focuses on your name. It's this selection and rejection process that establishes your sense of reality. It also establishes what you consider a "problem" and what you consider a "solution."

Modifying our brain filter isn't easy. It's even harder when those around us share similar beliefs and expectations. It's hard to see a solution when everyone else has labeled and accepted it as a problem.

This explains how Rat was able to see the solution we were unable to see. This happens in business, education, society... in every aspect of daily life. Reality is replaced by misguided labels and beliefs. It's like following a flawed road map instead of looking out the windshield at the actual road on which you're traveling.

When we believe how things should or shouldn't be, rather than how they are, we are living an illusion. The more we focus on illusions, the more we block out reality. Likewise, when we focus on problems, we block out solutions.

We can become so focused on "problems," we can't see

anything else. Look at this series of geometric shapes:

At first they appear meaningless. That's because most

people focus on the black shapes and ignore the white

shapes in between. When you focus on the white

shapes, the black shapes become less important and

suddenly, "SOLUTIONS" appear.

Turning problems into solutions requires that we adjust our perception, suspend our judgments, and remain open-minded to all possibilities. In other words, it means seeing reality for what it "really" is and for what it "really" isn't.

Since our brain filters through volumes of random data each moment, selecting and rejecting evidence to support our beliefs, we need to consciously define and focus our attention on what it is we are seeking.

Look at the following words and quickly say the actual color aloud (not the word).

pink   blue   green   yellow   green   yellow   pink

blue   green   pink   yellow   blue   yellow   blue

green   pink   green   yellow   pink   blue   pink

blue   green   yellow   green   yellow   pink   blue

If you're like most people, even this simple challenge requires effort to reprogram your brain. With practice, this task becomes easier once you focus more on the color and less on the actual word.

What you believe and focus on... becomes your reality. If you go out looking for trouble, you'll find it. If you focus on happiness, it will appear. Once you decide what you're looking for, your brain will go to work to find it and make it your reality. Whether your focus is on something positive or something negative, your brain will subconsciously gather evidence to prove it and make it your reality.

Remember, evidence that could disprove our beliefs is marginalized or blocked, while weaker or even false evidence is distorted or enhanced to support them.

Since labeling something helps make it so, why

not start labeling every "problem" as a "Pink Bat"?

While this may seem counterintuitive at first,

successful people have been seeing problems as

solutions since the beginning of time.

Pink Bats seem to emerge more frequently in

troubled times, when "problems" are abundant.

In math, when you multiply negative numbers, you

get a positive solution. The same often holds true

with problems (negatives) and Pink Bats (solutions).

When you take off the blinders and view the world through pink-colored lenses, it appears different. Your focus shifts from a world of problems to one filled with endless opportunities and solutions.

History is full of Pink Bat solutions and success stories. No doubt, the future will be, too. The real question is about the present. How many Pink Bats exist today? How many unseen, mislabeled Pink Bats exist in *your* life? Remember, every "problem" has Pink Bat potential, and at the very least, presents an opportunity for positive change.

On the following pages are some examples of

successful people and organizations that have

changed the world by embracing Pink Bat thinking.

In addition, I have provided a few scenarios to get

you thinking about some that might exist today.

If you want to learn more about turning problems

into solutions, or if you have Pink Bat ideas or

examples to share, please visit: mypinkbat.com.

Perceived Problem: As I write this sentence, the U.S. Census Bureau estimates the Earth's population to be 6.792 billion. It's difficult to imagine the amount of material—plastic, glass, aluminum, cardboard, paper, wood—this many people will use in a lifetime. Add to that the existing waste already generated by the billions of people that preceded all of us and you start to get an idea of the magnitude of this problem.

Many ideas were explored to manage this problem, but none solved it. That's because the focus was on the problem... not the solution. As a result, toxic landfills expanded. At some point it became clear... the landfill solution was a growing problem that was adversely affecting our planet in countless ways.

Pink Bat Solution: Recycle. By processing and repurposing used materials to create new products, recycling cuts down on toxic landfills and reduces the consumption of raw materials. In addition, it reduces energy usage, decreases air and water pollution, and lowers greenhouse gases as compared to virgin production. Recycling also creates new jobs and opportunities for many people. Since this solution is more sustainable, it holds great promise for future generations as well.

Today, recycling plays an important role in waste management... to think it was once an unseen Pink Bat.

Perceived Problem: For U.S. farmers in the eastern states, a cast-iron plow worked fine. But for farmers who tried using it to cultivate crops in the rich Midwest soil, it was a disaster. In fact, attempting to cut through tough prairie ground with a cast-iron plow was problematic to say the least. Trying to use one in the sticky rich soil without it getting clogged was nearly impossible.

Many knowledgeable people focused on this problem. The more they focused on it, the bigger it seemed to become. In time, most of them concluded the Midwest soil was too big of a problem and gave up.

Pink Bat Solution: After moving to the Midwest, a young blacksmith (an outsider) learned of this situation and began focusing on a solution. One day, as he walked to work, a glint of sunlight reflected off an old discarded saw blade. To the sawmill, this old blade represented a worthless, worn out piece of steel... a problem. To young John Deere, it was a beautifully honed piece of smooth steel... a solution. After pulling it from the junk pile, he took it to his shop and created a plow that worked great in the "problematic" Midwest soil.

Today, the John Deere Company supplies equipment to farmers throughout the world... and it all started with a discarded saw blade—a Pink Bat.

Perceived Problem: In 1942 when researchers were searching for a way to make clear plastic gun sights, they formulated a substance called cyanoacrylates. It didn't work. In fact, it was a problem... it stuck to everything... so they rejected it.

In 1951, the formula was rediscovered by a new team of researchers, but this time, rather than reject it, one of the scientists was intrigued with its bonding properties. By viewing it through pink-colored lenses, he saw it for what it really was... and by using his imagination... he began to see it for what it could be.

Pink Bat Solution: Cyanoacrylates made an amazing super glue... it bonded almost anything you could imagine! Paradoxically, when it was discovered that the formula also bonded human skin, its strength became a perceived weakness. To many, the potential dangers of this problem outweighed the benefits.

That is, until the U.S. military heard about it. Doctors in Vietnam were looking for a quicker way to suture wounded soldiers. This "problem" became a solution that saved many people's lives. This Pink Bat is still being used today in medical applications around the world.

Perceived Problem: The amenities were great,
but the elevators in my client's new office building
were extremely slow. This became a major problem.
Every day, frustrated and often angry crowds stood in
the lobby, complaining as they waited for an elevator
cab to arrive. The building's developer and management
team hired consultants to assess the problem and
even solicited tenants for ideas. Here were some of
the suggestions:

Add a couple more banks of elevators.

Make the doors open and close faster.

Stagger business starting and ending times.

Have visitors come during off-hours.

Everyone was so focused on the problem, no one was
able to see it as a solution... well, almost no one.

Pink Bat Solution: One morning I arrived to find a crowd (larger than usual), standing in the lobby. But instead of an angry mob, everyone was happily gazing up at the new video monitors that had been installed over the weekend. They were getting stock market information, checking the weather, and reading employee-related news. Amazingly, some people didn't even board an elevator when it became available.

With Pink Bat thinking, the perceived problem became a solution. People were no longer waiting for elevators. Disney discovered this solution long ago. Waiting can be a big problem... or a great way to entertain and inform guests.

Perceived Problem: Each day, restaurants prepare french fries, onion rings, fish, shrimp, and chicken... the list of deep-fried food possibilities is long. Breaded, battered or plain, the amount of used vegetable oil is staggering. Disposing of this messy waste is an expensive problem for restaurant owners.

In addition, our dependence on foreign oil continues to rise along with the prices at the pump. This is a perfect storm for a Pink Bat solution. Remember, when more than one problem is present, a Pink Bat is usually waiting to be seen.

Pink Bat Solution: When we change the label from used grease or vegetable oil to biofuel, the problem quickly becomes a solution. By focusing on the solution, it becomes clear that discarded vegetable oil is a valuable commodity. It can power cars, trucks, planes… and perhaps someday… space travel. Today, companies compete to collect used vegetable oil. This solution not only solves the restaurant owner's problem, but it lessens American dependence on foreign oil and reduces greenhouse emissions.

Think of the millions of gallons of used vegetable oil that were discarded over the years because it was seen as a problem. How many Pink Bat solutions like this are waiting to be seen right now?

Perceived Problem: In San Marcos, Texas, drivers have a problem keeping their car windows clean due to the unique dirt roads that locals call "caliche." The blend of limestone dust, gravel and clay creates a fine white dust that billows up and coats the rear windows of residents' automobiles.

For those focused solely on the problem, the solutions seem obvious... build more car washes, resurface the roads, or tell residents to avoid driving down them. But when you see things for what they are, and not what they're "supposed" to be, and then use your imagination (apply Pink Bat thinking)... "problems" look very different. That's exactly how Scott Wade approaches the situation.

Pink Bat Solution: As an artist, Scott views the dust not so much as a problem, but as a unique canvas solution for his artwork. Now instead of complaining about the dust, the town residents are clamoring for the opportunity to have Scott create some original art on their rear window.

On a somewhat related note, a friend of mine who owns a regional bank, has built several new branches. He's concerned because customers aren't using the drive-up windows as planned. I suggested he install a car wash so customers can get their car cleaned while making a transaction. My friend hasn't taken my advice... but it did get him thinking differently.

Perceived Problem: Simply put, Greeley, Colorado, smells. The odor of manure produced by the hundreds of thousands of cattle raised on the outskirts of town permeates the air.

Can you imagine living with this problem? My first solution would be to move. But that doesn't solve the problem for others... nor would it address an even bigger problem... greenhouse gas emission. You could stop raising cows. Considering I don't eat meat, that solution sounds perfect to me, and I'm certain the cows would concur. This would solve many other problems as well. But, no doubt, the farmers would find my solution problematic.

Pink Bat Solution: To entrepreneurs, this stench smells like an opportunity... better yet... a solution. While most people focus on a manure problem, others see a manure solution... a continual supply of renewable energy... natural gas.

One local cattle-feed operator is capitalizing on this perceived problem by fueling a gasifier (a large oven) with cow dung. As the dung bakes, the gases fuel the fire... and the heat powers the feedlot boilers.

This solution not only reduces energy costs, but by converting methane into carbon dioxide, it also addresses environmental concerns. Pink Bats exist everywhere... you just need to see (or smell) them.

Perceived Problem: The Internet! Yes, that's right. Information is power, and for some businesses, a lack of control over this information is seen as a major problem. Today, employees can readily communicate and share ideas with one another and the outside world—and vice versa. Social media sites like Facebook, Twitter, and YouTube, along with countless blogs, only add to this growing concern.

Keeping employees, customers... and the world... from openly discussing your products, procedures, or services, seems like an insurmountable problem. Still, many corporations try to block employees' access to the Internet and discourage them from participating in social networks. By using Pink Bat thinking, many other solutions begin to appear.

Pink Bat Solution: If we focus on a solution instead of a problem, we realize that the Internet can truly empower employees. Being connected puts you in a better place to provide solutions. Social networking can enable us to deliver great customer service, and by extension, build employee, customer, and brand loyalty. Transparency creates accountability and builds trust. Solution-based companies are better able to capitalize on employee insights and listen to customers.

Blogs and social media provide an opportunity to identify new ideas for creating products, and improving existing products and services. As social media evolves and the Internet expands, Pink Bat thinkers will continue to prosper.

Perceived Problem: Americans are obese. Not all, but many. This includes children, too. Along with obesity comes serious medical conditions including heart disease and Type 2 diabetes. With diets low in fruits and vegetables, and high in processed foods, meat, salt, sugar and white flour, it is easy to trace the problem's source. Add in the fact that many Americans lead a sedentary lifestyle and the problem becomes even more obvious.

Americans have another problem, too... the country's energy grid is outdated. Many people advocate natural gas, while others believe nuclear is the best solution. Some claim wind and solar are superior solutions because they're the most sustainable. As another alternative, consider this Pink Bat idea.

Pink Bat Solution: Turn obesity into energy. Rather than having kids sit at desks all day, let them learn on elliptical machines or stationery bicycles that are hooked up to a generator. Not only will this improve school spirit while saving the district money, but most importantly, it will create healthier and happier kids. By extension, students will learn about energy, the environment, finances, calories, food and health.

As added incentive, kids generating the most energy each month could be recognized for their contribution. Armed with knowledge and success, children would then educate their parents about diet and lifestyle. While these ideas may seem a bit far-fetched, they exemplify how Pink Bat thinking can be applied to unrelated "problems" to create new solutions.

Looking back, solutions seem so obvious. And the number of historic Pink Bats seems infinite.

We've all heard the story about how Isaac Newton was sitting under an apple tree when an apple fell on his head. Rather than considering this a problem, he saw it as a solution—the Universal Law of Gravitation. As with most historic stories of this nature, this one has probably been modified or created to make a point. Even so it exemplifies Pink Bat thinking. While most people would view this falling apple as a problem, Newton saw it as a solution. Then he let his mind wander... if the force of gravity affects apples, perhaps it affects the orbit of planets, too. Sometimes simple "problems" connect us to much bigger solutions.

Consider the buggy whip. A century ago, it was a viable business. That's because the main mode of transportation was a horse-drawn buggy. Then the automobile came along. For most manufacturers of buggy whips, this was perceived as a problem.

But what if buggy whip makers would have seen it as a Pink Bat instead... and found different uses for their expertise... or started creating new products to serve the "horseless" carriage market? Imagine the success they could have experienced. The Model T wasn't the problem. It was the buggy whip manufacturers' misguided focus that created their demise. Whether it's newspapers, banks, or auto manufacturers... we can all become blind if we focus on problems, grow complacent, or feel a sense of entitlement.

In life, everything changes. To find Pink Bats, you must change, too. Without seeing reality for what it is, and using your imagination to see it for what it could be, today's Pink Bats will remain unseen.

While it's fun looking back on historic Pink Bats, it seems more productive to look forward and find solutions that will work today and in the future. How many unseen solutions have you missed? How many Pink Bats are waiting for you to see them?

Each time you're presented with a "problem," you'll be reminded of the answer: For every problem there's potential for a Pink Bat solution.

While this book focuses largely on individual thinking, most Pink Bat solutions require teamwork. Unique ideas can create synergy when open-minded individuals listen to one another and contribute. It's easy to dismiss a new possibility, follow the status quo, or throw a wet blanket on a concept that doesn't conform to tradition.

How many times has a Pink Bat—or perhaps a fragment of a solution—been presented only to be killed for falling outside the accepted paradigm? Creating and maintaining a Pink Bat culture, where people are encouraged to share their unique insights, is more important than ever today. When people are afraid to share Pink Bat possibilities, everyone loses.

As this book goes to press in October, it would be remiss of me not to mention the "pink" connection to Breast Cancer Awareness Month. As I sit at my desk in Chicago this evening, several landmark buildings are lit with pink lights. Amidst this pink glow, the posters, the ribbons, and special events, we are all reminded of the importance of prevention, early detection, and treatment as we continue to search for solutions to save more lives.

For every problem, there exists a solution... and at the very least... an opportunity. But it takes an open mind to see it... and intelligence and imagination to create it. I am confident in time, a cure will be discovered. Perhaps it will be found by an outsider, or a novice who sees what others have missed.

My reasons for writing *Pink Bat* were to plant some seeds, capture your imagination, and inspire you to start seeing the world in a new light. I hope I've accomplished my objectives in some way.

You can live each day in a world filled with "problems," or rise each morning and embrace a world filled with unseen solutions... eager for you to find them. The decision is yours... both worlds exist. The one you choose is the one you will create.

If you want to learn more about turning problems into solutions, or if you have Pink Bat ideas or examples to share, please visit: mypinkbat.com

Michael McMillan has a well-deserved reputation for creative thinking and delivering innovative results. He founded a visual communications firm that attracted a *Who's Who* of international businesses, and his work has been recognized by major design, marketing and advertising organizations around the world.

Michael's direction on Michael Jordan's *New York Times* best-selling pictorial autobiography *Rare Air* established a new standard and niche in retail publishing, and led to several more award-winning coffee-table books, including *Mario Andretti*, *The NBA at 50* and John Deere's *Genuine Values*.

After twenty years of growth and success, Michael sold his firm to pursue new challenges and interests.

As an author, Michael shared his unique insight on creative thinking in his best-seller, *Paper Airplane: A Lesson for Flying Outside the Box*, which conveys a profound and lasting message about the power of innovation and the courage to take action.

Other works by Michael include:

The Power of Teamwork: Coauthored with former Blue Angels pilot Scott Beare, this compelling book explores key principles embraced by the Blue Angels.

The Simple Truths of Service: Michael worked with Ken Blanchard and Barbara Glanz to produce this moving book about the importance of heartfelt customer service. To date, the viral video Michael created has been seen by more than 10 million people.

The Race: Michael collaborated with Mac Anderson to turn a poem into a visually stunning book that stresses the importance of perseverance.

Michael's breadth of knowledge and experience, combined with his story-telling ability, makes him a much-sought-after public speaker. He connects with audiences of all ages, leaving them both motivated and committed to embrace a future of endless possibilities.

To learn more visit: michaelmcmillan.com

THE POWER OF Teamwork
Inspired by The Blue Angels
Scott Beare & Michael McMillan

212°
the extra degree

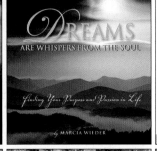
DREAMS
ARE WHISPERS FROM THE SOUL
Finding Your Purpose and Passion in Life
MARCIA WIEDER

You Can't
Send a Duck
to Eagle Sch
And Other Simple Truths of Le
Mac Anderson

The Dash

Great Quotes FROM Great Leaders
PEGGY ANDERSON

The Simple Truths of APPRECIATION
How each of us can choose to make a difference
Barbara A. Glanz

BY DAVID MCNALLY AND MAC A
EVEN EAG
NEED A PU
THE POWER OF ENCOURA

Audio CD Included
The STRANGEST SECRET
HOW TO LIVE THE LIFE YOU DESIRE
EARL NIGHTINGALE

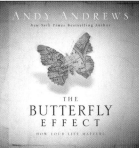
ANDY ANDREWS
New York Times Bestselling Author
THE BUTTERFLY EFFECT
HOW YOUR LIFE MATTERS

The Simple Truths of Service
Inspired by Johnny the Bagger
By Ken Blanchard & Barbara Glanz

The POWE
ATTITU
MAC AND
SUCCES

Paper Airplane
A Lesson for Flying Outside the Box
Michael McMillan

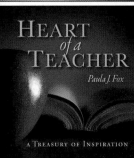
HEART of a TEACHER
Paula J. Fox
A TREASURY OF INSPIRATION

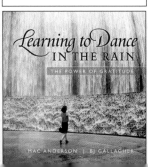
Learning to Dance IN THE RAIN
THE POWER OF GRATITUDE
MAC ANDERSON | BJ GALLAGHER

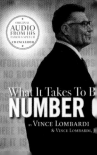
ORIGINAL AUDIO FROM HIS FAMOUS SPEECH
CD INCLUDED
What It Takes To B
NUMBER C
BY VINCE LOMBARDI
& VINCE LOMBARDI,

If you have enjoyed this book, we invite you to check out our
entire collection of gift books, with free inspirational movies, at
simpletruths.com

You'll discover it's a great way to inspire friends and family,
or to thank your best customers and employees.

We would love to hear how Simple Truths books enrich your
life and others around you. Please send your comments to:

Simple Truths Feedback

1952 McDowell Road, Suite 300

Naperville, IL 60563

Or e-mail us at: comments@simpletruths.com

or call us toll free...
800.900.3427

The End... is the start of a new beginning.